The DEFINITIVE guide to Cogent Liberal Talking Points

2020 Election Special Edition

By Kamala Warren

ISBN 978-1-7334381-1-7

Cover illustration by Gstudiomagen on Dreamstime.com

Disclaimer: After carrying out untold hours of exhaustive investigation with the intent of providing a definitive guide on the subject, it is to the best of the author's knowledge that all of the information presented in this is book is both accurate and properly attributed – hence, all of the pages are blank.

Saint Grobian Press

Shanghai – Tyumen – Urumqi – Pyongyang – Izhevsk - Danbury

Check out our other great products at:

www.UnionOfTruth.org

Other books by Kamala Warren:

1- The DEFINITIVE Guide to Facts and Logic that Justify the Mandatory Usage of Preferred Pronouns

2- The DEFINITIVE Guide to Facts and Logic that Justify Disarming Law-Abiding Citizens

3- The DEFINITIVE Guide to Fact-based Justification for Trump's Impeachment

4- The DEFINITIVE Guide to Facts and Logic that Justify Universal Basic Income

5- The DEFINITIVE Guide to Facts and Logic that Justify Having Co-ed Locker Rooms in Public Schools

6- The DEFINITIVE Guide to Trump's Treasonous Collusion and Obstruction

7- The DEFINITIVE Guide to Fact-based Justification for Homosexual Indoctrination of Kindergarten Students

8- The DEFINITIVE Guide to Fact-based Justification for Spying on Candidate Trump

9- The DEFINITIVE Guide to Trump's Hate-Filled Racist Remarks

10- The DEFINITIVE Guide to Democratic Party Accomplishments in the Trump Era

11- The DEFINITIVE Guide to Facts and Logic that Justify Government-Run Healthcare

Blank Page

The DEFINITIVE guide to Cogent Liberal Talking
Points

Blank Page

The DEFINITIVE guide to Cogent Liberal Talking
Points

Blank Page

The DEFINITIVE guide to Cogent Liberal Talking
Points

Blank Page

The DEFINITIVE guide to Cogent Liberal Talking
Points

Blank Page

The DEFINITIVE guide to Cogent Liberal Talking
Points

Blank Page

The DEFINITIVE guide to Cogent Liberal Talking
Points

Blank Page

The DEFINITIVE guide to Cogent Liberal Talking
Points

Blank Page

The DEFINITIVE guide to Cogent Liberal Talking
Points

Blank Page

The DEFINITIVE guide to Cogent Liberal Talking
Points

Blank Page

Blank Page

The DEFINITIVE guide to Cogent Liberal Talking
Points

Blank Page

The DEFINITIVE guide to Cogent Liberal Talking
Points

Blank Page

The DEFINITIVE guide to Cogent Liberal Talking
Points

Blank Page

The DEFINITIVE guide to Cogent Liberal Talking
Points

Blank Page

The DEFINITIVE guide to Cogent Liberal Talking
Points

Blank Page

The DEFINITIVE guide to Cogent Liberal Talking
Points

Blank Page

The DEFINITIVE guide to Cogent Liberal Talking
Points

Blank Page

The DEFINITIVE guide to Cogent Liberal Talking
Points

Blank Page

The DEFINITIVE guide to Cogent Liberal Talking
Points

Blank Page

Blank Page

Blank Page

The DEFINITIVE guide to Cogent Liberal Talking
Points

Blank Page

The DEFINITIVE guide to Cogent Liberal Talking
Points

Blank Page

The DEFINITIVE guide to Cogent Liberal Talking Points

Blank Page

The DEFINITIVE guide to Cogent Liberal Talking
Points

Blank Page

Blank Page

The DEFINITIVE guide to Cogent Liberal Talking
Points

Blank Page

The DEFINITIVE guide to Cogent Liberal Talking
Points

Blank Page

The DEFINITIVE guide to Cogent Liberal Talking
Points

Blank Page

The DEFINITIVE guide to Cogent Liberal Talking
Points

Blank Page

The DEFINITIVE guide to Cogent Liberal Talking
Points

Blank Page

The DEFINITIVE guide to Cogent Liberal Talking
Points

Blank Page

The DEFINITIVE guide to Cogent Liberal Talking
Points

Blank Page

Blank Page

The DEFINITIVE guide to Cogent Liberal Talking
Points

Blank Page

The DEFINITIVE guide to Cogent Liberal Talking
Points

Blank Page

The DEFINITIVE guide to Cogent Liberal Talking
Points

Blank Page

The DEFINITIVE guide to Cogent Liberal Talking
Points

Blank Page

The DEFINITIVE guide to Cogent Liberal Talking
Points

Blank Page

Blank Page

The DEFINITIVE guide to Cogent Liberal Talking
Points

Blank Page

Blank Page

The DEFINITIVE guide to Cogent Liberal Talking
Points

Blank Page

The DEFINITIVE guide to Cogent Liberal Talking
Points

Blank Page

The DEFINITIVE guide to Cogent Liberal Talking
Points

Blank Page

The DEFINITIVE guide to Cogent Liberal Talking
Points

Blank Page

The DEFINITIVE guide to Cogent Liberal Talking
Points

Blank Page

Blank Page

The DEFINITIVE guide to Cogent Liberal Talking
Points

Blank Page

The DEFINITIVE guide to Cogent Liberal Talking
Points

Blank Page

The DEFINITIVE guide to Cogent Liberal Talking
Points

Blank Page

The DEFINITIVE guide to Cogent Liberal Talking
Points

Blank Page

The DEFINITIVE guide to Cogent Liberal Talking
Points

Blank Page

The DEFINITIVE guide to Cogent Liberal Talking
Points

Blank Page

Blank Page

The DEFINITIVE guide to Cogent Liberal Talking
Points

Blank Page

The DEFINITIVE guide to Cogent Liberal Talking
Points

Blank Page

The DEFINITIVE guide to Cogent Liberal Talking
Points

Blank Page

The DEFINITIVE guide to Cogent Liberal Talking
Points

Blank Page

The DEFINITIVE guide to Cogent Liberal Talking
Points

Blank Page

The DEFINITIVE guide to Cogent Liberal Talking
Points

Blank Page

The DEFINITIVE guide to Cogent Liberal Talking
Points

Blank Page

The DEFINITIVE guide to Cogent Liberal Talking
Points

Blank Page

Blank Page

The DEFINITIVE guide to Cogent Liberal Talking
Points

Blank Page

The DEFINITIVE guide to Cogent Liberal Talking
Points

Blank Page

Blank Page

The DEFINITIVE guide to Cogent Liberal Talking
Points

Blank Page

The DEFINITIVE guide to Cogent Liberal Talking
Points

Blank Page

Blank Page

Blank Page

Blank Page

The DEFINITIVE guide to Cogent Liberal Talking
Points

Blank Page

The DEFINITIVE guide to Cogent Liberal Talking
Points

Blank Page

The DEFINITIVE guide to Cogent Liberal Talking
Points

Blank Page

The DEFINITIVE guide to Cogent Liberal Talking
Points

Blank Page

The DEFINITIVE guide to Cogent Liberal Talking
Points

Blank Page

The DEFINITIVE guide to Cogent Liberal Talking
Points

Blank Page

The DEFINITIVE guide to Cogent Liberal Talking
Points

Blank Page

The DEFINITIVE guide to Cogent Liberal Talking
Points

Blank Page

The DEFINITIVE guide to Cogent Liberal Talking
Points

Blank Page

The DEFINITIVE guide to Cogent Liberal Talking
Points

Blank Page

The DEFINITIVE guide to Cogent Liberal Talking
Points

Blank Page

The DEFINITIVE guide to Cogent Liberal Talking
Points

Blank Page

Blank Page

The DEFINITIVE guide to Cogent Liberal Talking
Points

Blank Page

Blank Page

The DEFINITIVE guide to Cogent Liberal Talking
Points

Blank Page

Blank Page

The DEFINITIVE guide to Cogent Liberal Talking
Points

Blank Page

The DEFINITIVE guide to Cogent Liberal Talking
Points

Blank Page

Blank Page

The DEFINITIVE guide to Cogent Liberal Talking
Points

Blank Page

The DEFINITIVE guide to Cogent Liberal Talking
Points

Blank Page

Blank Page